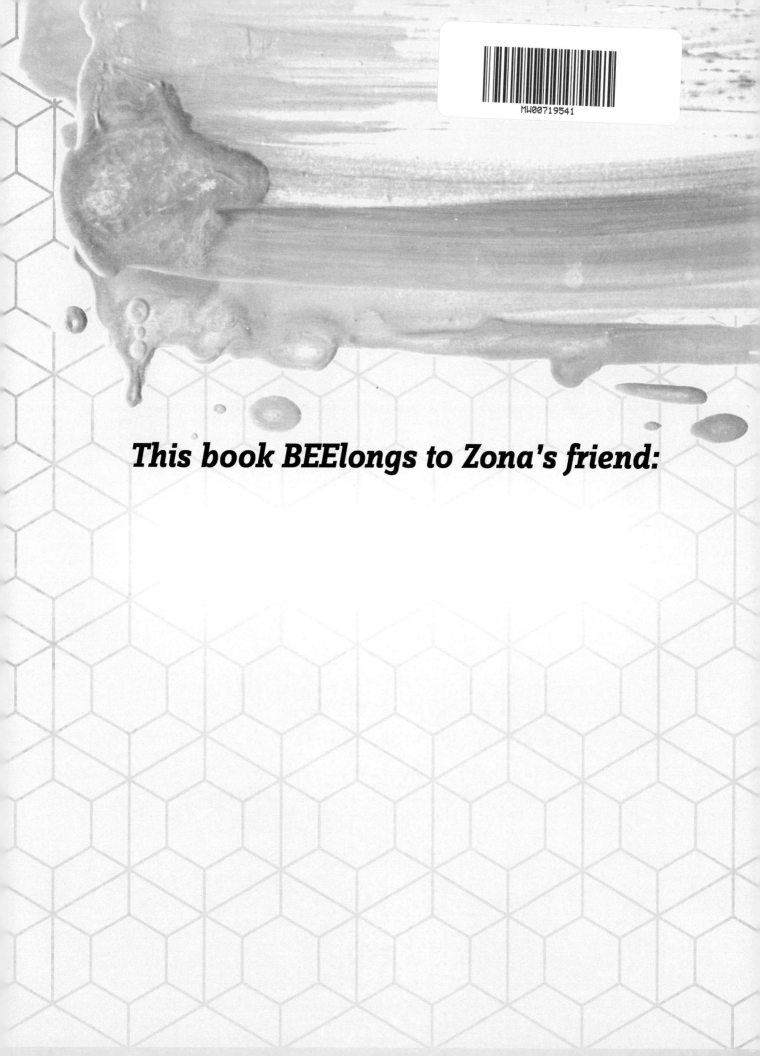

This book BEElongs to Zona's friend:

Dedications:

To Mom and Dad,
who demonstrated resilience and determination as global migrant
workers in pursuit of a dream. Mom, thank you for your love and support.
Your role as a social worker inspires me to seek justice for children.
Dad, your role as a software engineer and gardener inspires me
to be a good steward in both the digital and organic world.

To my mentor Steve Laug,
who walked with me through the shadow lands.
You shared stories that illuminated the dark path with
wisdom, insight, and hope. Thank you for coaching me to fearlessly pursue
my dreams and to always remember to "eat an elephant one bite at a time."

To my "beeloved" community of family and friends;
Your creative love and support is like honey to my soul.

Dave Farthing, Susan Ting, Carole Davis, Shannon & Erik Newby, Caron & John Smed,
Leeanne & Dallas Michayluk, Terri Boschman, Angelina Van Dyke, Diane Paulin
Jenny & Marty & Daniel & Jimmybob, Mindy Gross, Erica & Adam & Hannah & Benny Thomas;
Lukey & Ana Baldwin, Justine & Florence Hwang, Hailey Zheng, Maninder Dhaliwal,
Ginalina, Alphil Guilaran, Sam Raharjo, Patricia Marcoccia,
Breanne McDaniel, Charles Lin, Stephanie Ratcliff
My Toronto musical hive: Marco Bucci, Nathan Gerber,
JJ Gerber, Alyssa Bistonath, Kristian Podlacha.
My family in China: uncle An Su, aunties An Ming and An Wen, Annie and Calvin

Published by Sensing Stories in Vancouver, Canada, 2014
www.sensingstories.com
ISBN: 978-0-9918396-1-2

Zona
AND THE BIG Buzzzy Secret

Leah Yin 尹丽娅

Painted with beeswax!

The illustrations in this book are co-created with bees by means of using
pure beeswax mixed with colour pigment along with Chinese ink and rice paper.
The illustrations are further enhanced digitally on the computer.
No bees were harmed in the process of creating this book.
Let's be creative together! Discover more at:

WWW.ZZZONA.COM

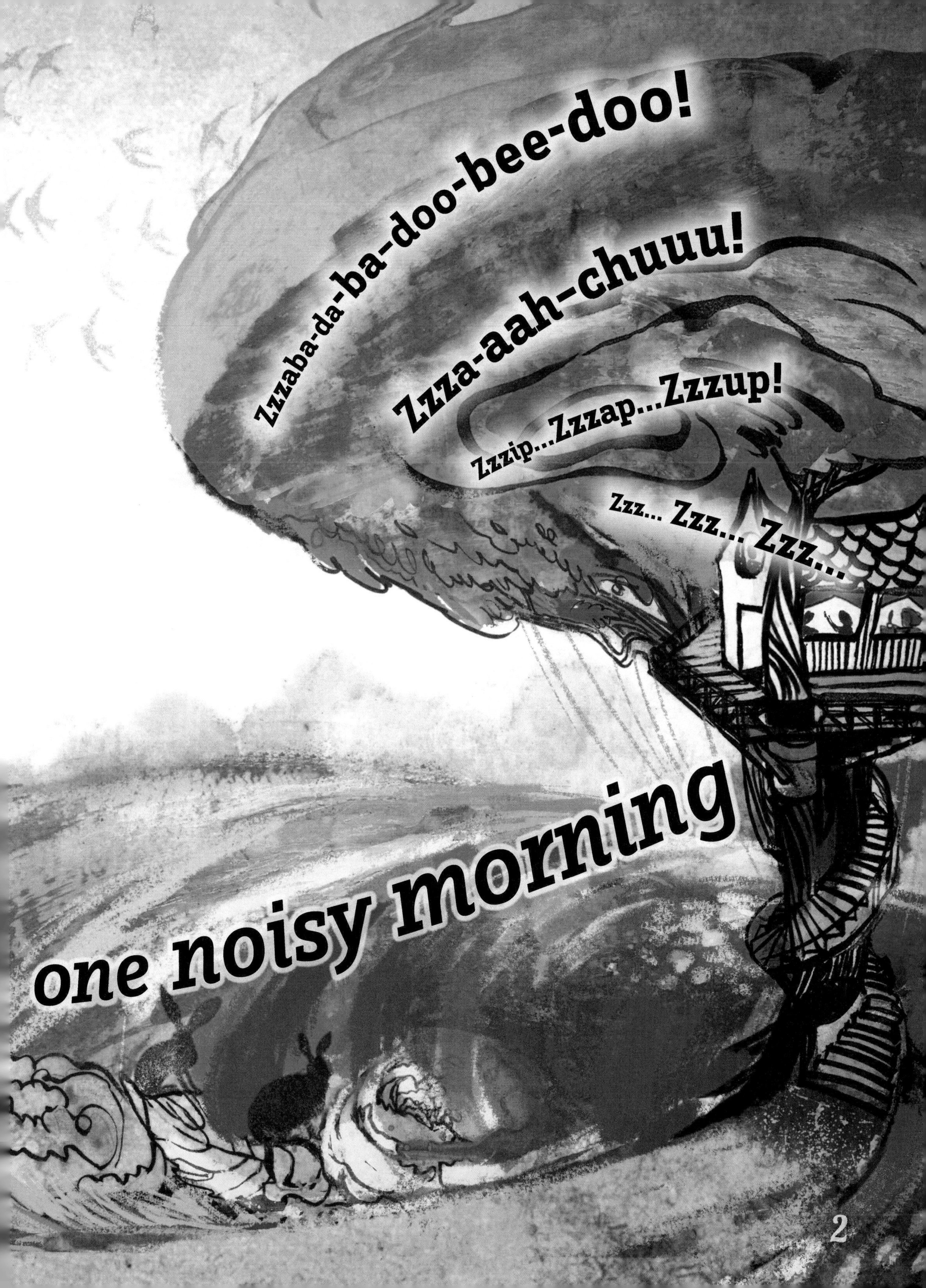

one noisy morning

Anybody want to doodle

Baba is busy fixing a new invention in the workshop...

Mama is busy studying a new flower in the lab...

with me please?

Grandma is busy cooking a new recipe in the kitchen...

Grandpa is busy daydreaming ...

A little later Zona...
Grandma is busy right now...

Zzz...Zzz...Zzz...

Not now Zona...
Mama is busy right now...

Soon Zona...
Baba is busy right now...

Zowzers! Look!
At least take a

Why is everyone always so busy?
Is anybody actually home?

And just doodle by myself...

Hmph!

8

Zowzers! Look at these big, puffy clouds...

Doodle With Zona...

What do you see in the clouds?

Zowzers! Look at these big red pomegranates!

These three pommies look like Chinese lanterns and those three look like big red monsters with lots of teeth!

Bzzz

Doodle some pomegranates with Zona...

...bzzz...bzzz...

Bzzz...Bzzz...Bzzz...

Hey, who's making that sound?

Doodle a swarm of bees...

Bzzz...bzzz...bz
Bzzz...bzzz...bzzz
Bzzz...bzzz...bzzz
Bzzz...bzzz...bzzz...
Bzzz...bzzz...bzzz...

Bzzz...bzzz...bzzz... Bzzz...bzzz zz...

I'm Zzzulu!

We're not trying to cause a fuss, but why are you ignoring us?

We are a big family of two hundred plus! We're curious about everything just BEE-cause!

I'm Zzzoni!

We swarm to discover the world around us!

Please show and tell! Let's buzz and discuss!

I'm Zzzarco!

What is YOUR name? Want to BEE friends?

Why are you holding a tree branch in your hand?

Well Zulu, Zoni and Zarco, you sure have a lot of questions!

To doodle, you first need to find something that you love to look at!

Then you need to find a special tool to capture what you see!

Everyone uses different tools to doodle. See here, I use my dad's special pen!

But **we** don't have any doodle tools Zona!

Hmmm, why don't you bees try swarming in the air to doodle a picture together?

zz...doooodle now!

Doodle your favourite doodle tool!

18

Now doodle this...

Bzzz...

Bzzz...

And doodle this...

20

Listen up doodle bees...

Are you ready to doodle something super tricky? Now doodle exactly what I tell you. Got it?

Got it...

Bzzz...

Doodle a big tall tree...

Under the tree is a big wide garden...

Bzzz...

Now doodle a winding staircase...

that goes up and around the trunk of the tree so we can climb from the garden to the top of the tree. Okay, now on top of the tree, doodle a tree house with a pointy roof...

24

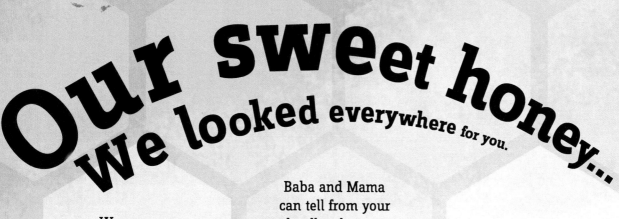

Our sweet honey...
We looked everywhere for you.

We are sorry
we were too busy
to play with you
this morning
Zona.

Baba and Mama
can tell from your
doodles that you
have discovered
amazing things
around you...

Sweet doodles Zona!
Grandma and grandpa
love to see
how *you* see the world!

Doodle Zona with Zulu, Zoni and Zarco!

Amazzzing to meet Zona's family! Sweet sight to see! Sweet as can bee!

A warm and buzzy hello to you...

Yah-bee-dah-bee-do-bee-dooo!

Mama! Baba! Grandma! Grandpa!
Can I tell you a big buzzzy secret?

I made friends with a swarm of bees and guess what... I taught them how to doodle!

Meet Zzzoni, Zzzulu, and Zzzarco!

Bzzz...Bzzz...Bzzz...Bzzz...

Bzzz...Bzzz... Bzzz.

Zowzers, look up!

doodled our family together!

28

Bee A Whole Family Activities:
Let's All Doodle Together...

Zowzers! Yes, indeed life can get buzzy and busy! Try to make some time to doodle and connect as a family everyday! Through doodling, each family member, young and old, will discover unique ways to express and share their feelings and ideas.

DOODLE FACE-2-FACE

Get everyone in the family to doodle each other and make a collection of home-made portraits! Feel free to doodle meaningful objects into each portrait to express more about the person!

DOODLE JAM SESSION!

Start your day doodling a smile! Get everyone to doodle a sunny face on their plate with breakfast ingredients!

OPEN AIR DOODLE!

If you live near a beach, or dirt patch, all you need is a stick and some earth and you've got yourself a great doodle tool and canvas! Get each family member to doodle something and have the rest of the group guess what was doodled!

Enjoy an intimate time of doodling together!

Bzzz...Bzzz... Bzzz...

Bee A Whole Family Activities:
Let's All Doodle Together...

Doodle what you see outside

Doodle a garden with plants & insects

Doodle yourself when you feel happy

Doodle yourself when you feel mad

Doodle yourself when you feel sad

Doodle yourself when you feel silly

IMAGINE...
Doodle each
of your family
members like
honey bees...

CPSIA information can be obtained
at www.ICGtesting.com
Printed in the USA
BVXC01n1958240614
357174BV00002B/4